Your Child with Autism is Speaking, Are You Listening

Secrets to Speaking the Language of Autism

Shawna Sparlin

This book is dedicated to my boys, Stephan, Shane and Braedan. You have brought joy, laughter and excitement to my life. I know that each of you has taught me more than I ever taught you and I will be eternally grateful. I love you all more than you will ever know.

Other Books by Shawna Sparlin

25 All Natural Cough & Cold Remedies

Younger Skin in 30 Days or Less

Eat Your Anxiety Before it Eats You

Magickal Life Series

Magick of Love (Book One)

Navigating the Land of Autism Series

Your Child with Autism is Speaking, Are You
Listening (Book One)

TABLE OF CONTENTS:

MY JOURNEY TO THE LAND OF AUTISM

Becoming a parent of a child with special needs is similar to planning a dream trip to a foreign land, for example, France. You spend months planning the trip, learning the language and packing your suitcases. You read books on the history and plan out an itinerary of all of the sites that you want to visit. Finally, the day arrives that you head to the airport and board the plane. You are so excited that your journey is beginning, and you look forward to all of the new experiences that are going to change your life.

Now imagine that in the middle of your flight, the stewardess announces that the plane is no longer going to France! Instead, you have been rerouted to Greece. Instant panic sets in as you know nothing about Greece. You have not studied the history, or learned the language and have no idea what you are going to do in Greece. Welcome to being a parent of a child with Autism! You have just been dropped off in an exotic, often chaotic, foreign land, and you need to learn the language in order to communicate with the natives.

Autism is a difficult country to navigate. No clear maps are available, and the language is different with each of the locals that you meet. When you first arrive you are likely to be afraid and frustrated by your lack of knowledge and ability to communicate.

None of the items that you have packed in your bags will help you to navigate this strange country. Do not be afraid, with time, and a lot of patience, you will learn how to find your way around and be better for the journey.

My voyage to the land of Autism began in 1987. I have been living in this new country for the last 28 years, and it is now my home. I love the locals and have learned far more from them than they have learned from me. I have learned a whole new meaning to the word patience. I have learned a language that most people cannot even begin to comprehend. I have learned the true meaning of the words compassion and unconditional love.

Allow me to be your travel guide. Whether you have just arrived or been here for a while, I would like to show you some of the sites. My goal with this book is to help you learn how to speak the language so that you can communicate with your Autism natives. Although the scenery may be different for each of us, the journey is much the same. I hope you find the information, and my personal stories, helpful in understanding and connecting with your child with Autism.

LOST AND CONFUSED IN A FOREIGN COUNTRY

Communication is what binds us together and without it every one of us is enclosed in our own private world. Without language or communication, we have no way to share our thoughts, ideas and no way to express our basic needs. Children with Autism have a difficult time expressing themselves verbally, and it is up to the rest of us to figure out a way to understand them. Children with ASD have a language of their own, we just need to learn how to speak it.

Imagine looking around you, and nothing of the world makes sense; in fact the world seems like a jumble of sounds and activities that you cannot understand. Worse, you can't seem to form the words to communicate that confusion to the people close to you. Welcome to the world of the Autistic child. If you thought that as a caregiver, life is hard for you, think how many times worse it is for these children who cannot in most cases communicate verbally?

Children on the spectrum tend to exhibit some odd behaviors that you will find troubling and baffling. Your child is not the only one who has a difficult time of communicating with you; you will find it difficult to understand them. I spent many years lost and confused and felt very much alone in this strange world. What I learned is that once you figure out how to speak the language and understand the culture, the journey gets so much easier.

My son Stephan introduced me to the land of Autism in 1987. He was a bright, happy baby. Stephan hit all of the normal milestones that the parenting books told me he would. When he was 18 months old, he had his MMR vaccination. Within one week, my bright, happy, cuddly son was gone. He quit making eye contact, quit playing with toys, and would not let me hold and cuddle him anymore. He began exhibiting strange behaviors, hand flapping, spinning in circles for hours on end and self-injurious behaviors like banging his head on the walls.

I remember thinking the faeries had come and stolen my son and left me one of their changelings. Up to this point, he talked just like any other child his age. After the shot, he lost all of his spoken words. I had no idea what happened or how to deal with this strange new creature living in my home. Like many parents, I tried to deny that anything was wrong with my son.

My daughter arrived in 1989. She was a beautiful, although demanding, baby. Unlike her brother, she needed constant attention and wanted to be held all the time. I used to take her to the pediatrician and demand to know what was wrong with her. He laughed and informed me that there was nothing wrong with her; she was a typical baby. When she started exhibiting some of her brother's strange behaviors, I knew that I needed to do something.

My pediatrician gave me a referral to the Child Development and Rehabilitation Center in Portland, Oregon. Stephan and I spent four, very long, days there. After numerous, extensive tests, they called us back in to give me the news. The doctor told me my son had Autism, here's a pamphlet, have a nice day. Then we were sent on our way.

The pamphlet was a joke. It didn't give me any information on what Autism was, what I was supposed to do now or where to go for help. Unfortunately, this is still the type of treatment that most parents receive when their child is diagnosed with ASD. I wish I could give you all of the answers that you are looking for, but I am still learning as I go.

I did what I always do when I want to find answers to my questions, I went to the library. At this time, there were not as many books on the subject as there are now. The first book I found on Autism kept referring to the "refrigerator mother" syndrome. The author blamed the condition on a mother's lack of bonding with her child as an infant so the child withdrew from the world. Since Stephan had been developing normally up until 18 months of age, I knew this was not the answer. I returned the book to the library and continued my search to find the answers I needed.

Unfortunately, I was not able to find much information on Autism at this time. I spent many years making it up as I went. Not only did this make life difficult for me but it must have been horrible for my son. We spent many days with him screaming or banging his head on the walls and me in tears. For a parent, it is very difficult to see your child in pain and not be able to fix it for them.

I knew my son was there, somewhere; I just needed to figure out a way to reach him. I spent hours on the floor trying to see the world from his perspective. Talking to him, reading to him and just being in his face in an effort to prevent him from withdrawing into himself. Our world changed when our interpreter showed up.

Katrina began talking when most other children do. She was very attached to her brother and loved him completely. One day I observed them communicating in what sounded like gibberish to me. Katrina would come to me and tell me things like, "Mom, Stephan wants a drink of water". I would ask her how she knew that. She would reply because he told me so then look at me like I would know this if I weren't so stupid. It turns out that she was usually right about what Stephan was saying or wanting.

Although Stephan seemed unable to speak, my children had developed their own language and would communicate with each other. At last, I had an interpreter! This jibber-jabber made it possible for Stephan to communicate his wants and needs with myself and his relatives, as long as Katrina was around to interpret for him. During this time, I was also able to begin translating some of his cues and form an idea as to what he was wanting or needing. I cannot tell you how wonderful this was and how it changed our world.

My second tour guide, Shane, arrived on February 9, 1999. In the fourth month of the pregnancy, I had a routine ultrasound done. The technician informed me I was having a boy, and I knew then and there that he would be Autistic. I voiced my concerns to my doctor and he told me not to worry, the chances of having more than one child with Autism in the same family were extremely high. My doctor told me I had a better chance of winning the lottery or being struck by lightning. I sure wish I had bought a lottery ticket then!

Shane was a beautiful, happy, gentle boy. But I knew from the beginning that he would be diagnosed with Autism before he was three. He began exhibiting interesting behaviors when he was eight months old. He never babbled as a baby or was interested in games like peek-a-boo. He began sitting on his own at ten months, and that is when the spinning began.

One day I walked into my kitchen and found Shane sitting in the middle of the floor. He was surrounded with lids from the baby food jars all spinning; there must have been eight or ten of them. He would not only spin round objects, but anything he could find;

books, hairbrushes, cars, etc. I was amazed at what he had taught himself to do.

Shane never did speak but after all of the years of research and raising Stephan, I was better equipped to understand nonverbal communication. By this time, I had learned to read their body language and the benefits of a routine and picture schedule (more on this later).

I gave birth to Braedan, on November 21, 2002. He did not have an easy time of it. My older children were not happy that another baby was coming. The pregnancy was difficult, and so was his birth. He was so very different from his brothers that I held out hope that he would be a per se "normal" child (whatever that is).

From the time Braedan was an infant he reminded me of a little old man. He always had the most serious look on his face. He had sensory issues with his feet; he could not stand to have anything touching them. He did not crawl until he was twelve months old, and then he did it with his feet in the air. He almost never smiled, and I never heard him laugh or giggle until he was two years old. I knew from an early age that Braedan too was another one of my travel guides.

Our world has never been easy, but neither has it ever been boring. I do not know why I was lucky enough to have three sons all with Autism, I will never know this. What I do know is that they changed my life in many profound, unexpected and beautiful ways. Over the past 28 years, I have learned more than I thought I wanted to know on the subject and will try to share that with you in the chapters to follow.

GETTING THE LAY OF THE LAND

One of the fascinating things about the Land of Autism is the scenery is constantly changing. Some of the landmarks where I live may be the same, similar or completely invisible to many of you. In my region, every day is a new day. In the 28 years that I have spent living here I can honestly say that I have never been bored. In this chapter, we will explore what Autism is and what it isn't. I will share some of the facts, as of this writing, and some of the myths surrounding Autism. I cannot give you a clear map, but I can help you to find the landmarks that are common to your region.

I will not go into great detail, as there are already many books written about what Autism is and the theories of what causes it. For the purposes of this book here are the simplified definitions of what Autism is and isn't.

What Autism Is –

Autism Spectrum Disorder (ASD) is a developmental condition that causes extensive social, communication and behavioral challenges. Autism is a spectrum condition in that it affects children in different ways. One of the biggest challenges that autistic children and their families face is communication. Right from birth, babies communicate by listening to people's voices, reacting to noise and many other ways that let you know they are aware of external stimuli. Children with ASD, on the other hand, may seem distracted and unaware that somebody is speaking to them. They don't imitate people as a way of learning as other children do.

Children who have ASD also have great difficulty in interpreting gestures and facial expressions. For example, you may smile or wave at a child with ASD, and they have no idea what it is that you're trying to communicate. Children with ASD have a difficult time feeling empathy for people around them.

Children on the spectrum spend twenty-four hours a day, seven days a week, on sensory overload. Their brains do not know how to block out what is important and what is not. They find it very difficult to navigate our loud and often confusing world. This sensory overload is the main reason your child withdraws, rocks in a corner or exhibits challenging behaviors.

To get an idea of what living with Autism is like, watch this short video Sensory Overload
http://tinyurl.com/ld5mzw7

What Autism Is Not –

Autism is not a disease. It is not contagious, and there is no known "cure". Many effective treatments and interventions exist that can help children with Autism. Unfortunately, these programs are not one-size-fits-all. What works for one child, may not work for others.

Autism is not the same as mental retardation (I really hate that phrase). Nor is it similar to any other child developmental disability. With most developmental disabilities, the child will be able to learn but will hit a plateau where their development stops. With Autism, there is no plateau, children on the spectrum are capable of learning just like you and I. Sometimes is just takes them longer.

Autism is not your fault! After receiving this diagnosis, many parents spend their time agonizing over what they did to cause their child to be Autistic. This burden of guilt can be debilitating and interfere with the work that you need to do. Unpack your bags and get off the guilt trip. There are many theories as to what causes Autism, but nothing that is concrete.

Autistic children are not mean children. Although their behavior may seem aggressive at times, they are often overwhelmed and have no other way to communicate this. They are not, by nature, bullies or mean-spirited. It's easy to label a child with ASD as being rude or badly behaved. If you try for a moment to wear their shoes, then you'll have a better understanding of why it all gets to be too much for them. They can be disruptive and aggressive but more often than not, it is a sign of confusion and frustration.

Autism Myths –

According to Autism Speaks, here are the biggest misconceptions surrounding Autism:

Myth: People with autism don't want friends.

Truth: If someone in your class has autism, they probably struggle with social skills, which may make it difficult to interact with peers. They might seem shy or unfriendly, but that's just because he or she is unable to communicate their desire for relationships the same way you do.

Myth: People with autism can't feel or express any emotion—happy or sad.

Truth: Autism doesn't make an individual unable to feel the emotions you feel, it just makes the person communicate emotions (and perceive your expressions) in different ways.

Myth: People with autism can't understand the emotions of others.

Truth: Autism often affects an individual's ability to understand unspoken interpersonal communication, so someone with autism might not detect sadness based solely on one's body language or sarcasm in one's tone of voice. But, when emotions are communicated more directly, people with autism are much more likely to feel empathy and compassion for others.

Myth: People with autism are intellectually disabled.

Truth: Often, autism brings with it just as many exceptional abilities as limitations. Many people with autism have normal to high IQs, and some may excel at math, music or another pursuit.

Myth: People with autism are just like Dustin Hoffman's character in Rain Man.

Truth: Autism is a spectrum disorder, meaning its characteristics vary significantly from person to person. Knowing one person with autism means just that—knowing one person with autism. His or her capabilities and limitations are no indication of the capabilities and limitations of another person with autism.

Myth: People who display qualities that may be typical of a person with autism are just odd and will grow out of it.

Truth: Autism stems from biological conditions that affect brain development and, for many individuals, is a lifelong condition.

Myth: People with autism will have autism forever.

Truth: Recent research has shown that children with autism can make enough improvement after intensive early intervention to "test out" of the autism diagnosis. This research is more evidence for the importance of addressing autism when the first signs appear.

Myth: Autism is just a brain disorder.

Truth: Research has shown that many people with autism also have gastro-intestinal disorders, food sensitivities, and many allergies.

Myth: Autism is caused by bad parenting.

Truth: In the 1950s, a theory called the "refrigerator mother hypothesis" arose suggesting that autism was caused by mothers who lacked emotional warmth. This theory has long been disproved.

Myth: The prevalence of autism has been steadily increasing for the last 40 years.

Truth: The rate of autism has increased by 600% in the last 20 years. In 1975, an estimated 1 in 1,500 had autism. In 2009, an estimated 1 in 110 had an autism spectrum disorder.

Myth: Insurance covers therapies for people with autism.

Truth: Most insurance companies exclude autism from the coverage plan and only half of the 50 states currently require coverage for treatments of autism spectrum disorders.

Autism Facts –

According to the National Autism Association, here are the most recent facts on Autism:

Autism is a bio-neurological developmental disability that generally appears before the age of 3.

Autism impacts the normal development of the brain in the areas of social interaction, communication skills, and cognitive function. Individuals with autism typically have difficulties in verbal and non-verbal communication, social interactions, and leisure or play activities.

Individuals with autism often suffer from numerous co-morbid medical conditions that may include: allergies, asthma, epilepsy, digestive disorders, persistent viral infections, feeding disorders, sensory integration dysfunction, sleeping disorders, and more.

Autism is diagnosed four times more often in boys than girls. Its prevalence is not affected by race, region, or socio-economic status. Since autism was first diagnosed in the U.S., the incidence has climbed to an alarming one in 68 children in the U.S.

Autism itself does not affect life expectancy. However research has shown that the mortality risk among individuals with autism is twice as high as the general population, in large part due to drowning and other accidents.

Currently there is no cure for autism though, with early intervention and treatment, the diverse symptoms related to autism can be greatly improved and in some cases completely overcome.

Autism Facts & Stats

Autism now affects 1 in 68 children.

Boys are four times more likely to have autism than girls.

About 40% of children with autism do not speak. About 25%–30% of children with autism have some words at 12 to 18 months of age and then lose them. Others might speak, but not until later in childhood.

Autism greatly varies from person to person (no two people with autism are alike).

Comorbid conditions often associated with autism include Fragile X, allergies, asthma, epilepsy, bowel disease, gastrointestinal/digestive disorders, persistent viral infections, PANDAS, feeding disorders, anxiety disorder, bipolar disorder, ADHD, Tourette Syndrome, OCD, Sensory integration dysfunction, sleeping disorders, immune disorders, autoimmune disorders, and neuroinflammation.

Autism is the fastest growing developmental disorder, yet most underfunded.

A 2008 Danish Study found that the mortality risk among those with autism was nearly twice that of the general population.

Children with autism do progress – early intervention is key.

Autism is treatable, not a hopeless condition.

HOW AUTISM AFFECTS COMMUNICATION

Parents and guardians usually notice that something is just not right with their children between the ages of two to three years or even earlier. Suddenly you'll realize that your beautiful child is not responding to you and seems to withdraw into his or her own world.

People being people, will bombard you with their opinions that will probably add to your confusion. Some will tell you it's just a slight delay, and your child will catch up soon enough. Others will make you want to rush to the ER with their panic-inducing diagnoses.

Parents have reported observing different and sometimes even strange behaviors from their little ones inconsistent with older siblings or children of friends or relatives. Some of these behaviors and habits that give parents an inkling that something is not right with little ones include:

•Meltdowns that can be brought on by something simple like turning off the TV

•Fascination with objects like toys rather than with people

•Speech delay

•Late in reaching milestones

•Flapping hands and shaking the head over and over again

•Lack of eye contact

•A fascination with lining things up

•Intolerance for loud noises

•Sleeping for only a few hours

•Doesn't smile when smiled at

•Doesn't respond to his/her name

•Does not like cuddling or touching

•Does not copy or imitate your movements or facial expressions

•Appears to be in his own world

SIGNS AND SYMPTOMS OF AUTISM IN OLDER CHILDREN

•Appears disinterested in other people and surroundings

•Inability to make friends

•Does not know how to behave in social situations

•Inappropriate behavior like touching people, standing too close

•Does not talk about feelings or seems not to understand what feelings are

•Does not bond with others through shared interests

•Prefers not to be touched or hugged

For every child with Autism, they have some problems in three key areas:

-        Verbal and nonverbal communication

-        Social interactions

-        Flexibility in things and behavior

AUTISM DIAGNOSIS

Autism Spectrum Disorder (ASD) is diagnosed using behavioral tests as there's no medical test for the condition. Instead, Doctors and other health professionals carry out assessment tests based on the child's communication, social interactions and their interests.

It is a difficult condition to diagnose due to the wide range of unique symptoms, challenges and abilities that affects different children with ASD. It is a worrying time for parents wanting to know what is wrong with their child, however, as devastating as it is to have your child diagnosed with ASD, it is far better to know early. With an early diagnosis:

•There's access to services aimed at helping your child

•There's also access to financial help from the government and other agencies

•A sense of relief that finally your child can get the help that they obviously need, and you also learn how to support your child.

Some of the assessments to determine if your child has ASD may include:

-       A detailed physical examination to ensure that your child is not suffering from another medical issue that may be causing symptoms similar to those of ASD.

-       Focused observation that means a series of appointments so that your child can be observed. The health professionals will want to assess your child's interaction with other children, their cognitive ability, language and general behavior.

-       A medical assessment may include:

•Developmental milestones

•Sensory investigation

•Medical history of the mother's pregnancy and birth of the child

•Family history of genetic disorders

•Eating and sleeping habits

It is a detailed and complex process to correctly diagnose ASD. It's important to follow it through so that as a parent and a caregiver, you can provide the support that your child requires to thrive and be independent.

Because Autism is a spectrum of disorders, meaning that its effects are different in every person or child, the effects on communication skills are just as varied. One child may be completely non-verbal while another may speak but not understand the meaning behind the words.

Let's look at the common communication issues that you may observe in your child who has ASD.

INABILITY TO UNDERSTAND BODY LANGUAGE

Children with ASD typically do not understand body language, for example, they cannot tell if somebody is angry or happy. They don't get facial expressions and tone of voice. Some examples of an inability to read body language include:

-        Standing too close or too far from people. They are not aware or conscious of the right space to have when you're talking to someone or standing next to someone.

-        Inability to read facial expressions

-        Making eye contact – Children on the Autistic spectrum find it difficult to maintain eye contact.

Maintaining eye contact takes away their concentration of what the speaker is saying. Adults with ASD have explained how eye contact causes them to strain, that's why they tend to look at other parts of the face like the mouth.

SENSES WHICH ARE OUT OF SYNC

Children on the spectrum find it difficult to process sensory information. What is ordinary to you is painful or uncomfortable for them.

Some may experience hyper sensitivity to sounds. For example, a child on the spectrum may not be able to stand to hear somebody singing or the sound of a vacuum cleaner or the whirling of a washing machine. Everyday sounds are painful for them. Going to crowded places like malls becomes impossible for children with ASD.

While other people tend to block out other noises and concentrate on a conversation, children or adults on the spectrum are bombarded with all the noises in the environment and are unable to block out the irrelevant noises.

For another child, it may be intolerance for fluorescent lights. An exposure to these lights may cause a meltdown and the child may suffer from headaches and other discomforts. The hum that fluorescent lights produce is disturbing for children with ASD and the flickering of the light distorts their visual perception and distracts them from other activities.

Other children have a heightened sense of smell, for example, going into a deli can result in the child throwing up.

When children on the spectrum become tired or fatigued, it worsens their sensitivity to sensory stimuli. They might be able to tolerate a certain level of noise early in the day but when they get tired, their tolerance decreases significantly.

EXPRESSIVE LANGUAGE

Many children with ASD have a problem expressing themselves, for example, they may know the answer to a question but they cannot get the word out at that instant. Therefore, it is important for parents and caregivers to provide other alternatives like multiple choices, visual cards or the use of pictures etc.

They also may not have the word to express how they're feeling. That's why it's important for parents and other caregivers to be alert for other forms of communication from the child.

CONVERSATIONAL ISSUES

Some children on the spectrum may experience difficulty in sustaining a conversation. They tend to talk in a monologue that does not involve anybody else. They can talk for hours about a certain favorite subject but are not interested in another person's views. Children and adults on the spectrum tend to talk about their favorite subject without a point being made at the end of the monologue.

Their speech may even seem incoherent but most likely it is because an ASD sufferer may fail to provide background information making the speech difficult to understand.

NON-VERBAL CUES

Children on the spectrum often do not pick up on tone of voice or a comment with a hidden meaning. Because of this, they are vulnerable to bullying at school. They go along with the teasing and bullying from other children because they don't read into the negative meaning behind the words.

Regular children are aware of rude and vulgar words that you're prohibited from saying. A child with ASD is not aware of these words. Other children may teach an ASD child these vulgar words and derive fun from hearing the child with ASD repeat them inappropriately. It is crucial as a parent or caregiver to pay attention and be on the lookout for a child on the spectrum who is being bullied and act on it before it gets out of hand.

READING AND WRITING

Many children with Autism are visual learners. Thus, many may have problems writing or others have sloppy or ineligible handwritings. Other children on the spectrum may know their alphabets very well and even be able to read. However they may fail to understand the purpose of the story or the moral behind stories may be lost on them.

Thus some children may read very well but they may not understand what it is they are reading about.

Children with ASD also tend to have special interests, for example, Johnny who is on the spectrum loves trains. He should therefore be encouraged to read about trains, after all, the purpose is to learn how to read and understand what you're reading.

For children with ASD, learning the alphabet is very easy and is not a struggle to them. For a parent or caregiver, the focus should not be in memorizing the alphabet; rather it should be to understand the words in stories and the messages behind the story. It is also important for these special children to understand the importance of learning how to read and write.

Other tips for teaching children on the spectrum to read and write are:

- Many children with ASD have tactile sensory issues and do not like the feel of a pen or crayon their hands. These sensory issues make it difficult, if not impossible, for these children to write.

- Avoid long winded verbal instructions

- Autistic children are good at drawing and computer programming, encourage them in their areas of strength

- Understand that Autistic children cannot control their bad handwriting. Let them type instead.

LEARNING TO SPEAK AUTISM

Learning the language of Autism is a lot like learning to speak Chinese. No one language exists for the whole country. Different regions have different dialects. The same is true of Autism. As we learned earlier, only 60% of the people with Autism ever communicate verbally. The remaining 40% use some form of non-verbal communication. It is your job as a parent or caregiver to learn how to translate this non-verbal communication.

Only one of my sons was verbal, Stephan. At the age of ten he spoke to me! We were sitting on the couch watching his favorite cartoon. I had my head in his lap as he liked to play with my hair. Out of nowhere he leaned over, looked me right in the eye and said "Love you Mom". Then went back to watching TV like this was no big deal. I almost fell off the couch. He spoke and he said he loved me, I cried for weeks over this huge development and the memory still brings tears to my eyes.

Stephan spoke a strange language of Echo-English and visual cues. In the region where Shane was from they spoke Shanish; a combination of jibber-jabber sounds and gestures. Bradean spoke Braedanese; a mixture of gestures, his very own sign language and visual cues. Each of my sons did learn how to communicate with me but in their own ways. This is likely to be true of your child. Once you figure out what works for them you can teach others how to understand and communicate with them as well.

When you work with children on the spectrum you have to teach them that words have meaning. Here are some tips to help you accomplish this feat:

Giving Words Meaning

Most of us have seen the Peanuts cartoons by Charles M. Shultz. Remember when the grownups were talking? You never actually see them but instead hear something like "waah wah waah". When your child with ASD is young, this is how you sound to them. Many of them are not able to recognize the noise you are making as words or language. To them it is just one more noise that is assaulting their senses. You need to teach your child that this noise has meaning.

First, be mindful of the words you are using. Do not ask a question if you are not willing or able to live with their answer. It took me some time to master this. I used to ask Stephan if he wanted to get dressed. Of course he always answered no as he loved to be naked. So then I was stuck at home for the day as it is not socially acceptable to go around town in just your underwear. I had to train myself to say things like, "Stephan, it's time to get dressed now".

Children on the spectrum interpret language literally. When you use common phrases and language, this is what they understand.

WHAT YOU SAY & THE MEANING TO A CHILD WITH ASD

You say: It will be a walk in the park (easy to do)

They understand: You or them will be taking a walk to the park

You say: I'm all ears (I'm listening)

They understand: You're made of ears

You say: It's raining cats and dogs (it's raining)

They understand: Cats and dogs are falling from the sky

You say: Something is a piece of cake (easy to do)

They understand: There's a cake somewhere nearby

You can imagine how perplexing the environment is for a child with ASD when people tell you that they are all ears and you can clearly see that they only have two. Or that you're in hot water, and you are standing on the living room floor.

"You left a dirty cup in the sink" to a child with ASD is a statement. They may not understand that what you mean is that they should go and wash up the dirty cup. They are not able to infer meanings from statements therefore you need to be direct and state what you need done clearly.

Speak clearly to a child with ASD and save your sarcasm and idioms –they are lost on the child. Speak in plain words and say exactly what you mean so that the child with ASD can understand your meaning.

Avoid using slang when speaking to your child. Don't say things like "that's so dope", this phrase will only confuse them and has no meaning to them.

Always, always follow through on what you tell them. If you tell them you are going to get ice cream after dinner, you MUST go and get ice cream after dinner. It doesn't matter if someone drops by to visit or the phone rings. Your child will not care and your words will have no meaning without actions to demonstrate them.

People with Autism love details but get lost with big concepts. I used to get so jealous of other parents around the holidays. Those parents of neurotypical children can get away with things like, "If you don't mind me, Santa won't bring you any presents". This type of threat holds no weight with our children. Santa Claus is a concept and so is the Easter Bunny and the Tooth Fairy.

Use short, concrete sentences and be specific with the words you choose. People on the spectrum tend to think in pictures, not words. If you want them to pick up their shoes on the living room say, "Pick up these shoes and put them in your room". Just saying pick up your shoes is not specific enough. In their minds they are likely picturing every pair of shoes they own, or you own or they have seen on TV.

When your child begins to understand that the noise coming from your direction has meaning, communicating starts to get easier. They will learn to listen for your voice and distinguish it from all of the other noise around them. If you are very lucky, they will begin to use language themselves.

Echolalia

Although my son Stephan did start talking at the age of ten, that does not mean he was very good at conversation. When he was agitated or very excited about something he talked very quickly and it was hard to understand what he was saying. He also tended to use echolalia most of the time.

Echolalia is a condition associated with Autism where your child repeats words or phrases that they've heard over and over again without knowing the meaning behind the words or phrases. For example, you may ask your child a simple question such as 'Susie, you want some juice?' and instead of answering they'll repeat exactly what you asked and in some cases, imitate your voice and tone.

It may seem rude but your child doesn't mean to be rude. It's their way of communicating their needs to you. It is also a sign that your child can learn a lot more with the right help. In other words, it's a positive sign that they are capable of much more.

A child with ASD may also have a tendency to memorize large parts of a favorite video or movie and keep repeating it over and over again. Children with ASD tend to have a lot of anxiety since a lot of their environment may not make sense to them. They must therefore develop ways to cope with that anxiety and if repeating phrases over and over again helps them to calm down, then by all means let them do so without making an issue out of it.

The tone that a person uses tells a lot about what they mean and their feelings. Some children with ASD tend to speak in a parrot like robotic voice making it difficult to read emotions and feelings behind the words. For parents and caregivers, it becomes difficult to understand what they mean or what they need because their tone doesn't reflect their feelings.

So because their caregivers don't understand what they want or need, children with ASD tend to be physically aggressive and rough, grabbing things rather than politely asking. If they could, they would ask politely, but they don't have the social and communication skills that we take for granted. The good news is that with patience, your child can be taught to communicate in a better way.

ALL BEHAVIOUR IS A FORM OF COMMUNICATION

After 28 years I could give you a ton of examples of challenging behaviors but one memory sticks out in my mind. I had one of those days planned to take care of business; shopping, pay the bills, get the oil in the car changed, etc. Throughout the day Stephan just screamed and screamed and no matter what I did I could not figure out how to make him stop. By the end of the day we were both beyond tears and completely frustrated. At one point I even yelled at him to just stop screaming already.

I did manage to complete most of my errands that day. Although we dealt with many stares and so-called advice on how to discipline my child to make him better behaved. While I was getting him ready for bed that night I discovered the reason behind all of the screaming. He had stepped on a thumbtack and it was sticking through his shoe into his foot. I felt like the worst mother in the world. What kind of mom screams at their child when they are in pain?

When I related this incident to the pediatrician, he did his best to make me feel better. He pointed out to me that a per se "normal" child would have found a way to tell me of the pain in his foot. They would have pointed at their foot, walked with a limp or not walked on it at all. Stephan did none of these things and really, checking a child's foot for a thumbtack during a meltdown, is not a parent's first thought.

Over the years, I have learned a lot about challenging behaviors, meltdowns and their triggers. One of the things I have learned is that all behavior, good and bad, is a form of communication. Once Stephan began talking, he could tell me when he didn't feel well or something hurt. My younger boys, however, never communicated verbally so I had to learn how to distinguish the meaning behind their behavior. Seventy percent of the time a challenging behavior was due to hunger. One way that I learned to avoid these behaviors is to feed them more often throughout the day and to let them "graze" as needed.

Many parents take offense to my using the word "graze". They automatically think of a herd of cows in a pasture somewhere and do not want to equate that with their child. But grazing accomplishes a number of things for both the child and the parent. Snacks are readily available when the child needs them, thus eliminating behaviors. Using a variety of textures encourages oral stimulation and exploration that are necessary for encouraging vocalization. And it helps the child to make choices for themselves which is important for everyone.

Grazing is simple to do. I used a muffin tin filled with different textured food and left it on my table. Shane only liked to eat soft food and Braedan liked crunchy things. I would fill each section of the tin with healthy snacks they liked as well as different textures for them to try. For example, you can use goldfish crackers, fruit (if leaving it out for the day use dried fruit to prevent spoiling), nuts and cubed cheese. Learning to figure out the meaning behind your child's behavior takes time and creative thinking skills.

Many children on the Autism spectrum do not speak or tend to use very few words. That's not to say that they do not communicate because they do, through their behavior. Children on the Spectrum do not use words to express their needs or wants; instead they use behavior to communicate, whether they are aware of it or not. So for non-verbal children, behavior is indeed communication.

For example, a child on the spectrum may retreat to a corner, perhaps to get away from too much stimuli and that's their way of communicating that the environment is too much for them to handle.

It is difficult as a parent of an autistic child to view behavior as a way of communication rather than misbehavior since most of the behavior of a child on the spectrum is challenging. However this shift in mindset is important if you are to effectively parent your child with Autism.

That's not to say that it's easy. It is difficult to cope with challenging behavior from a non-verbal child.

Once you're able to view your child's challenging behavior as a form of communication, then you're already on the way to understanding your child.

TRIGGERS OF BEHAVIOR ISSUES ON CHILDREN WITH AUTISM

More often than not, there's a reason behind that maddening behavior and it may take a while to figure it out. Children on the spectrum don't do things just to annoy you or drive you crazy. Remember that they are not very good at reading body language and facial expressions. As you grow progressively annoyed at something that your child with autism is doing, keep in mind that they cannot tell that you're upset.

Since they cannot read your body language, it's therefore your job to read their behaviors and interpret them to figure out what your child may be communicating.

Here are some possible reasons behind the outbursts and meltdowns.

1.   Sensory stimulation

We mentioned this earlier where children with ASD get overwhelmed by sensory information which leads them to release this overload through disruptive behavior. For example, the fluorescent light in a classroom may be causing agitation to a child with

ASD. That child may throw a tantrum and the teacher may fail to understand the cause of the meltdown.

Or your child may become aggressive when you go shopping together, throwing things or engaging in self-injurious behavior. This could be due to over stimulation of the senses, like too much noise, too many people, too much movement etc.

2.   Sensory sensitivity

Children with ASD can be hypersensitive (over sensitive) or hyposensitive (under sensitive) to some of the five senses.

The good news is that over time this sensitivity decreases and parents also learn to deal with them, however while it is happening its very distressing for the child.

The physical signs of sensory hypersensitivity in a child with ASD include:

•Extreme distress in response to high pitched or loud noises.

Sometimes these noises are every household noise like the flushing of the toilet, the humming of the fridge, a train track nearby, singing children, the cacophony of the streets or malls etc.

•A low threshold for pain.

The child may seem to over react to a little pain but to them the pain is a lot. A tiny injury may cause an unending screaming fit in an ASD child who is hypersensitive and you may even label your child a drama queen or drama king.

•Bothered by fabrics and certain textures of clothes and labels.

Children who are sensitive to touch cannot tolerate starchy clothes which in addition to irritating their skin, makes a scratchy noise every time they move. It's a noise other people would not notice but to the ASD child who is sensory sensitive, it is as loud as a truck accelerating.

•Get distressed when somebody touches them especially when the touch is unexpected.

They resist hugs even from people who are close to them. Parents may interpret this disinterest in physical manifestation of love like hugging as a lack of desire to be affectionate. However, ASD children just don't like being touched and especially without warning and they don't associate physical touch with love.

•The child may be fussy about food and only eat foods of a certain color or texture.

Sometimes this problem of eating can become so severe that it becomes an eating disorder. Children with ASD take picking food to a new level. They limit themselves to four or fewer foods, causing a lot of distress for the parents.

One child might decide he or she will only eat yellow or white food, while another will only eat crunchy food, leaving a very small choice of foods which suit their palate.

The biggest issue with the foods that they pick is that they are not nutritionally balanced. They may contain a lot of carbohydrates and calories but no fiber leading to another problem of constipation.

The physical signs of sensory hyposensitivity in a child with ASD include:

•A high tolerance for pain.

Some ASD children have a very high tolerance for pain, for example, your child may bang his head into a wall and not complain about the pain, yet there's blood trickling down and has obviously been hurt. As a parent, you may have a hard time knowing when a child with a high tolerance for pain is sick because they may not complain of the pain but may act up in other challenging behavioral ways.

•A love for spicy food and cannot distinguish food that is too hot.

•May hurt other children when playing

•May like bright colors

•The child with ASD might not feel cold in the winter and want to wear shorts and vests

•An obsession like need to rub hands against certain textures

3.   Acting deaf

Because of their hypersensitive senses, children with ASD act deaf. You talk to them and they behave as if they cannot hear you. When hearing tests are done, they come out normal. Your child's hearing is just fine. The reason behind this behavior is that a child with ASD has learnt to block out sound as they can't process both sound and sight. So they block out one sense to avoid an overload.

4.   Seizures

Seizures can begin at any age in a child with ASD and are thought to be caused by brain abnormalities which disrupt neurons and cause changes in the activities of the brain. Seizures can be difficult to differentiate from the normal behavior of children with ASD. Some of the signs that a child with ASD is having a seizure include:

•Severe headaches

•Confusion

•Baffling staring spells

•Stiffening of muscles

•Twitching of the facial muscles

•Jerking of the limbs

•Unresponsiveness

•Shallow breathing

•Loss of bladder or bowel control

•No recollection of the seizure episode

5.   Transition time

Your child with ASD may find it difficult transitioning from one activity to another. Children with ASD find it difficult to change their attention from one thing to another. It causes them stress and they may react by engaging in challenging behavior.

They're also prone to self-imposed routines that they follow and you may not be aware of them. So when you rush them from one activity to another, you throw confusion into their routine.

Your ASD child may also have a compulsion to finish any task that they begin so when you cut off activities without a warning, you rob them of the opportunity to finish what they were doing.

6.   Social triggers

Children with ASD get anxiety over social situations that they know that they can't cope with. For example, your child may have a melt down every time they have to go for recess in school. Just like other children, your child on the spectrum has a need for friends and when he can't make friends, it becomes a distressing period for him.

HOW TO AVOID AND DEAL WITH THE TRIGGERS OF BEHAVIORS

1.   Sensory sensitivities

Sensory problems are a big cause of behavioral issues in children with ASD and because they may not communicate that discomfort, it's up to you as the parent to figure out what may be causing such distress to your child.

Here are some suggestions of how to help your child deal with sensory issues.

a)   Use of head phones and ear plugs

Doctors don't recommend the use of head phones and earplugs all day on a child with sensory sensitivities; however, they can provide some relief for an hour or two. The reason for this is that the child may become over dependent on them. Choose headphones with foam to baffle the sound that is causing distress to your child.

b)   Safe places and environments to visit

Make a list with the help of your child, if possible, of the different places you can visit together where their sensory sensitivities are not irritated. These places could be:

•A library

•A park

•A museum

•A quiet nature walk

•Church services

c)   Provide a quiet place

Have a safe place in a room where you child can retreat to when it all gets too much for him or her. This is a prevention strategy that will prevent a meltdown which will happen if the sensory overload continues.

Make this space attractive with a rocking chair or a beanbag chair where they will feel that they are separate from other activities going on in the room.

This space should be near enough so that when the child feels ready they can join the rest of the family or even the class.

d)   Transition time

Children on the spectrum have a great need for predictability. They dislike disruptions and a sudden change of activity can lead to a meltdown which manifests itself through tantrums. They need a transition period between activities. Below are some tips to help in transitional ASD children from one activity to the next.

•Make the end of an activity clear – Children with ASD don't like leaving things unfinished. So to signify that a particular activity is over, have a way to signify the end. For example, have a box where they can place the completed picture or a picture schedule where there's a drawing of the finished activity and they can tick it off.

•Make a schedule – This is a written list of activities that the child will partake in during the day. It should be complimented by pictures as most children with ASD are very visual and they learn and remember visually. A schedule is useful as a transition aide because the child feels prepared for every activity that will come up. In other words, their day feels predictable just the way they like it.

•Give plenty of time for transition – Nobody likes to be rushed and more so children or adults on the spectrum. Give your child plenty of time to adjust to a changing activity by telling them in good time about a pending change and what will happen. Provide continuous reminders at intervals. This will lessen the apprehension that your child feels when a change is looming.

•Minimize transitions –Transitions are stressful for your child, so the best strategy is to minimize them. Plan your day early so that you can anticipate transitions and figure out ways to eliminate them. For example, if you have planned several different activities for a day and you notice that your child is not coping very well, reduce the activities to five. Or if changing clothes is an issue, reduce the number of times that your child has to change clothes in a day.

•Use a timer – For children with ASD, time is an abstract concept that is difficult to understand. A timer is visual and it will help the child see how much time is left for that activity.

e)   Desensitizing

A gradual exposure to the noise which distresses your child is a great way to help them overcome that sensitivity and get used to the noise. For example, if you live near a main road and the sounds of cars disturb your child, you can start by opening the window just a little bit and over several weeks keep opening it a bit more. By doing this, you're letting the child gradually get used to that noise. Over time you can even open the door. It takes a lot of effort and patience but the alternative is even worse – a meltdown every time they cannot cope with that noise.

2.   Showing affection

Parents of children with ASD get distressed because their children refuse to hug and kiss. They even throw tantrums when people close to them insist on hugs. For a parent who wants to show affection to their child, it is heartbreaking when the child pushes you away or throws a tantrum because you want to hold them.

Don't take this refusal personally, instead understand and look for other ways to show affection without offending the child. Some of these ways are:

•Open your arms and let him make the choice if he wants a hug or not. If he doesn't, don't be hurt, the important thing is for the child to know that your arms are open for him when he's ready.

•Give him thumbs up and a wide smile to let him know that you love him if he doesn't want a hug.

•Ensure that people who are in close contact with your child such as teachers and caregivers are aware of his no hug policy to avoid meltdowns.

3.   Social triggers

Find out which social situation is triggering the challenging behavior. As with the example cited earlier of a child having a meltdown when it's time for recess, you can address this issue by explaining this to your child's teacher. Your teacher can then explain your child's problems to the other kids and get them to help him overcome this. When you're open about issues, people tend to get onboard and are willing to offer you whatever help you need especially when the issue involves innocent children.

4.   Sources of pain

Your nonverbal child may not tell you that they're in pain. By observing them you can put two and two together and figure out where the pain is coming from. For example, if your child has curled himself into a fetal position or into a ball, then it's highly likely that they may be having some stomach pain or discomfort.

5.   Seizures

Researchers estimate that nearly a third of all children with ASD get seizures caused by epilepsy. It is important for children with seizures to be correctly diagnosed as this can lead to poor health for that child or even premature death.

If as a parent you suspect that your child maybe having seizures, tell your doctor or health provider your concerns and they can have your child stay overnight in a hospital so that they can run an EEG on the child.

If it is confirmed that your child is suffering from seizures, the doctor will prescribe anti-epileptic drugs which will minimize and even prevent seizures.

BASIC STRATEGIES FOR COMMUNICATING WITH YOUR CHILD

Learning to speak Autism takes time and a great deal of patience. Each child on the spectrum is different and unique. I had three sons with Autism who were all very different. I had to learn and develop many different forms of communication for each son. My best advice is to not get frustrated, easier said than done, and never give up.

Autism affects communication in different ways, one child may become verbal over time, another never quite masters verbal communication. Whichever the case is, you can adopt some strategies to help your child learn how to communicate.

1.   Use short and simple sentences

'Ben, shut the door' is a better sentence to tell your child rather than,

'Come on Ben, we don't want the rain flooding the house, do we?'

Autistic children don't get complex sentences or instructions that end with a question.

2.   Give your child time to respond to a question

We are wired as human beings to ask a question and expect the answer immediately. Children on the spectrum however take time to process any information that they receive. To make matters more complicated, their facial expressions do not reflect that they are pondering on the question. You may mistakenly think that they did not hear you, when in fact they just need you to be a bit more patient and give them time to respond.

If you keep repeating the question and pushing them for an answer, what you'll get is a meltdown when they start to feel frustrated and overwhelmed.

However, if you practice giving them time after a question, it will pay off eventually when you notice that your child is taking less time to respond to a question. So keep going, it's difficult but it will be worth it in the end.

3.   Exaggerate your gestures and tone of voice

Use your hands when speaking to your child and a tone that exaggerates the situation so that over time your child can understand gestures and tone of voice. You should also encourage some eye contact by holding out objects near your eyes and even squatting to the eye level of the child. Don't force it because they tend to feel distressed by eye contact, just a little at a time that can build up with practice.

4.   Avoid negative words

Your child may have come to associate negative words with change which is unwelcome. Words like no, not now, stop and others may act as triggers for challenging behavior.

Use positive words even when you're at your wits end, which can be frustrating when your child appears to be ignoring you. By using positive words, like 'let's do this now…' you minimize the risk of a meltdown.

5.   Use your child's interest to foster communication

Children on the spectrum tend to have an almost obsessive interest in a certain subject or object. Use that to form the basis of communication by getting books about it and reading together and also letting them talk about that subject. This will help to build up their communication skills.

6.   Break up instructions into steps

Children with Autism tend to get lost in long verbal instructions. Break the instructions into simple steps giving your child ample time to absorb one step before moving on to another.

"We'll go to the library today after which we can go to the park and feed the ducks."

That sentence is too much for a child with ASD as it's too much information at a time. Break it up into steps and reinforce it with pictures showing what activity will follow which one.

7.   Use an even voice to communicate

No matter how angry or frustrated you feel, you must keep your tone even and not shout at your child. With non-autistic children, the technique of increasing the volume of your voice may work to curb inappropriate behavior but with a child on the spectrum it will worsen the situation. Remember that your child may also have sensitivity to noise, so increasing the volume of your voice will lead to a meltdown which you're trying to avoid as much as possible.

8.   Use childish language to communicate

Children remember the meanings of words when you use their childish version of it. For example, when describing a certain food, you could say 'it's so yummy...' rather than saying it's tasty or delicious.

9.   Imitate and copy your child

Mimic positive behavior, for example, if your child is playing with a toy car and making sounds of a car moving, copy his actions and the sounds that he's making. This will encourage interaction and also encourage the child to copy you too. Children with ASD do not instinctively learn by copying and mimicking, so you must teach them to do so. Remember not to copy negative behavior, only copy the positive behavior.

10.   Consider visual supports and devices

Visual supports and devices will help in the development of your child. They will improve communication by helping your child communicate their needs and desires. These devices also:

-       Improve their social skills

-       Increase attention span of children with ASD

-       Improve self-help skills

-       Improve academic skills

The reason why visual supports and devices work so well with ASD children is because most of them think in pictures instead of words. They process visual information faster rather than verbal which is too abstract for them.

It is also important to combine visual devices with written words to enable the child to make a connection between the word and the picture or video.

These visual devices and supports could be anything from clipboards, manila file folders, photo albums, photographs, highlighted tape to tape recorder, timers, calculators, simple voice output devices and more complex devices like computers, cameras and voice output devices.

While my son Stephan did start talking at the age of ten, he was never the greatest conversationalist. He would spend hours talking my ear off about the Power Puff Girls, or one of his other favorite cartoons. Yet, if I asked him how his day at school was he would become agitated or have a meltdown. But at least he was able to communicate his basic needs and wants with me which makes life in the land of Autism much easier.

My younger sons are not verbal. On a rare occasion I have heard both of them speak but only when they are completely upset and frustrated. I have spent many a sleepless night crying and agonizing over ways to make their lives easier. I cannot even begin to imagine what it must be like to go through your day and not be able to communicate with anyone. Having to watch a child you love more than life itself live this way is very difficult for a parent.

Up to now I have discussed various ways to give words meaning and given you strategies for communicating with your tour guide. All of these tricks will work with both verbal and nonverbal children. In the next chapters, I will be showing you different methods that exist for helping your nonverbal child to find his or her voice.

SIGN LANGUAGE

Research has shown that children with autism greatly benefit when they learn sign language because it's visual and it provides a way to easily communicate. Sign language also stimulates the development of speech and language. Teaching your ASD child to sign has many benefits and some disadvantages.

WHAT ARE THE BENEFITS OF LEARNING SIGN LANGUAGE

1.   Children who learn sign language are also able to speak at a faster rate.

 It appears as though as the child learns sign language, an area of the brain dedicated to speech is activated. Most signs used in sign language are visually associated with the objects that they refer to. In this way, a child with ASD learns that every object has a name and is able to associate each object with its name.

2.   Reduction or elimination of challenging behavior.

The inability to effectively communicate is what causes most of the challenging behaviors in children with ASD. In fact, this inability to communicate is what makes it so difficult for the child to express a need or desire. However, once they learn to communicate through sign language, these challenging behaviors decrease because there's a way to communicate needs and feelings.

3.   Increased social interactions

When a child with ASD learns to sign, it increases their interaction with others because it's a way to connect. Communication skills are vital for social interactions and learning sign language increases a child's confidence and ability to socialize.

4.   Sign language builds cognitive structures

Sign language helps to develop cognitive skills which help the brain to encode language leading to speech development. Encoding helps a child to learn and learning opens up a whole new world for children.

5.   Helps children with ASD communicate without verbal speech

Because many of these children cannot express themselves verbally, sign language is a wonderful way for nonverbal children to communicate even if they cannot speak.

6.   Sign language is portable and easily used anytime

It requires no set up; the communication is immediate as long as both parties understand sign language.

THE DISADVANTAGES OF SIGN LANGUAGE

1.   Sign language may not work with every child on the spectrum as it is highly dependent on the abilities and attention span of the child. Sign language requires a child to be focused and most children with ASD have a very short attention span.

2.   Sign language is not familiar to most people and while it may help a child with Autism communicate with the people close to him (who have learnt sign language), that child may still be isolated from other people who don't know sign language. Many people who will come into contact with the child like relatives, family friends, and the staff at the doctor's office etc. don't know sign language.

I did not use sign language with Stephan but did use it as one method of communicating with both Shane and Braedan. I bought a book on learning American Sign Language that had a lot of pictures in it. Using hand-over-hand, which is the method I used to teach them most of their everyday skills, I began trying to teach my boys to sign.

Shane had a difficult time with many of the signs as he had poor fine motor skills. The first sign that he picked up was the sign for "more". However, he did it in such a way that it took a while before I realized that was what he was saying. Shane would approach me and take my hands and use them to sign "more". None of his teachers knew what he was doing until I was able to explain it to them.

The first sign that Braedan learned to use was the sign for "stop". Once again, he did it differently and I had to figure out what he was saying. Braedan would clap his hands together for "stop". Braedan has always been my most stubborn and determined child of the three. When he was younger, he would get mad at me and follow me around the house clapping his hands. It took me quite a while to figure out that he was telling me to "stop".

Both Shane and Braedan learned other signs as they grew older. But they would only use them by manipulating other people's hands. Teachers and speech therapists alike did not have an answer as to why that was. Then, like a lightbulb going off over my head, I realized what I had done wrong. While teaching the boys to sign I used hand-over-hand. I took their hands in mine and demonstrated the sign I wanted them to learn. I believe in their minds they understood this to be the correct way to use sign language. When they wanted to sign a word they would take other people's hands and use them to form the sign. (I never said I was the sharpest tool in the shed.)

Creating Your Own Signs

Many children with Autism learn to use sign language effectively. Others, not so much, as it requires a lot of fine motor skills. A lot of these children use signs that are not included in the standard American Sign Language, and this is ok too.

When Shane was two I wanted him to have a way to say "I love you". I would take my hand and caress the side of his face while saying "Mommy loves Shane". Then I would repeat the gesture, using his hand to caress my face while saying "Shane loves Mommy". One day when he was about five, he crawled up into my lap, looked me in the eye and caressed my face. Such a happy day as another one of my sons had told me he loves me!

You can create your own form of sign language if you want to. The key to remember is that once your child masters the sign you will need to let the other people and caretakers in their life know what it is.

THE PICTURE EXCHANGE COMMUNICATION SYSTEM

Stephan started early intervention services through the public school system when he was three years old. The night before he started I was a nervous wreck. Would they take good care of him? Would he miss me? Would they be able to understand him? Know when he was hungry, thirsty or needed to use the bathroom? So many questions and so few answers.

I was reading a book by Temple Grandin at this time. I remember her talking about people with Autism being visual thinkers and that pictures were easier for them to understand than words. I went to a pawn store and bought a used Polaroid camera and a bunch of film. I started taking pictures of everything, the foods Stephan liked, the activities he enjoyed, and his favorite toys and books. I put all of the pictures into a small scrapbook and showed him how to use this to communicate. At this time I did not know that there was a formal system available for children on the spectrum.

The Picture Exchange Communication System (PEC) was developed in 1984 by Lori Frost, MS, CCC/SLP and Dr. Andrew Bondy as a way for autistic children to communicate nonverbally.

Children with ASD are taught to communicate their needs, observations through the use of pictures. Children are taught to exchange a picture or the real object for example, if the child wants an orange, he'll give an adult a picture of an orange.

PECS goes on to teach children to form full sentences through the use of the pictures. You can purchase a PECS package or cut off pictures from newspapers and magazines.

THE SIX PHASES OF PECS

Phase one

This is the initial phase and here the trainer finds out what the child finds interesting, for example a train, a ball, a type of food; anything really which captures the child's attention. The next step is to find a picture of that object and show it to the child. This is the phase where the trainer initiates communication by teaching the child that showing that picture results to him or her getting that object.

Phase two

Here, the trainer expands the use of the picture by having the child make a request but in different settings. This phase also teaches the children to be persistent communicators and to have the skills to obtain attention.

Phase three

By now the child has learnt to request an object with a single picture. In this phase, children are presented with two or three pictures of their favorite objects. This introduces the concept of choice to the child and enables them to pick what they want or need. Here is where it gets tougher and a lot of patience is required from the trainer as the level of difficulty increases.

Phase four

This phase introduces sentences with the use of sentence strips to the child. Sentence strips are a combination of words and pictures. For example, a child will take a picture of an orange and add the words I want.

Phase five

The trainer helps the child to formulate questions and requests. Here they are also able to answer the question what do you want?

Phase six

This is the phase where a child is taught how to make comments in response to such questions such as what do you hear? What do you see? What is it?

The PECS system is one of my favorite tools for nonverbal children. No matter where your child is on the spectrum they can learn to use some form of PECS effectively. Most of the schools teaching ASD children use it so there is consistency between school and home. If your school is not using it yet you can request that they do so during your next IEP meeting.

Purchasing the complete PECS system along with the necessary materials to use it can be quite expensive. Not only do you need the pictures but you will need scrapbooks, construction paper, Velcro, etc. The materials needed will depend on the type of tool you are creating for your child. If you cannot afford the PECS system you can create your own version of it. Use pictures from magazines or take them yourself. If you are a creative person, and have the time, you can draw them yourself as they consist of simple stick figures and line drawings.

For example, I glued a picture for eat and drink onto colored construction paper. Then I cut them out and laminated them. I applied a Velcro sticker to the back of the cards and to my refrigerator. I kept the pictures for eat and drink where my children could reach them and taught them to bring me one when they were hungry or thirsty. This is just one example for using PECS.

I also use them for creating their daily schedule. Children with Autism do not always understand the concept of time. Using a picture schedule helps them to see what their daily routine looks like. A schedule is a great way to help them transition between activities and reduce meltdowns throughout the day. Your daily schedule can be as simple or as elaborate as you like as long as your child understands its purpose.

You can purchase the complete set or smaller sets of the pictures used in the Picture Exchange Communication System here:

http://www.pecs.com/

COMPUTER USE: KEYBOARDING

Keyboarding can open up a new world of communication with ASD children. A success story of keyboarding is the story of Carly Fleischman, a thirteen year old girl with Autism. For many years, she could not communicate at all and she was diagnosed with severe autism. Doctors did not think her intellectual capabilities would develop more than those of a child.

She seemed in her own world most of the time, her hands flapping and in constant motion.

One day when she was eleven years old and working with her therapists, she felt sick and desperate to let them know what was happening, she went to a computer and typed out the words hurt and then help.

She started to type and out came this intelligent, sassy girl who was aware of her surroundings and environment. She started to have conversations with her family members through keyboarding and she has also helped parents to understand their autistic children by explaining some behaviors.

For example, she has been asked why Autistic children cover their ears and flap hands, and rock and hum? Carla answered "It's a way for us to drown out all sensory input that over loads us all at once. We create output to block out input."

So for Carla and other children with ASD, keyboarding can be a lifeline helping children communicate their thoughts, needs and desires.

DIFFICULTIES THAT AUTISTIC CHILDREN FACE WITH HAND WRITTEN WORK

•Poor handwriting – Many Autistic children have poor handwritings and researchers are not entirely sure why this is so, though there's a belief that their brain works much faster than their hands can keep up with, hence the poor handwriting. It's also blamed on sensory difficulties and poor motor skills.

•Sloppy work -Some children with ASD write very slowly, almost as if they're drawing every letter, others write big numbers and letters across the page, canceling out some and generally ending up with very sloppy work. They have no regards for appearance of the work and will write letters on top of others.

•Inertia – Children with ASD hate writing by hand and this can cause a child to completely refuse to write and even cause a meltdown. This inertia is thought to be caused by a part of the brain that resists activities which the child deems very difficult.

•The process of writing requires organization, sensory processing and motor control all of which are problem areas for a child on the spectrum.

•Difficulties of language also make it difficult for the child with ASD to come up with ideas on what to write about and arrange them in a sentence that makes sense.

BENEFITS OF USING THE COMPUTER FOR AUTISTIC CHILDREN

1.   Children who learn to use a computer show an improvement in other skills unrelated to the computer skills that they know.

2.   Teaching children with Autism requires a lot of patience and when the computer is used for lessons, it works very well because it does not get tired of repeating instructions and information over and over again.

3.   Children learning on computers focus for longer periods of time. Children on the spectrum show more curiosity to lessons provided via the computer than they do on a book.

4.   Children with ASD are drawn to the computer because they are predictable and the child feels in control. These children prefer to deal with inanimate objects where there will be no surprises.

5.   Errors are easily rectified unlike when the child is working on a book and the work becomes messy due to the many errors and corrections made.

DISADVANTAGES OF COMPUTER USE

1.   Autistic children love computers and there's a risk of them developing an addiction to the computer. There's also a risk of that child getting isolated from society. Parents must be careful so that computers don't replace real life relationships. You should restrict computer use to an hour a day and place the computer in a communal place.

2.   It encourages repetitive actions which are not beneficial to the child at all. A child with ASD is already prone to repeating actions over and over again and the computer can encourage this particular trait. Parents should watch out for this and always be aware of what your child is doing on the computer.

DEVICES TO ASSIST A CHILD TO ACCESS THE COMPUTER

A standard computer may need to be adjusted in order for a child on the spectrum to be able to use it. Below are some devices that help ease the way into the computer world for Autistic children.

1.   Big keys keyboard and Keys plus keyboard

It is an alphabet keyboard designed especially for children. The keys are an inch and color coded so as the child can find it easier to locate different letters and numbers.

Keys plus keyboard is arranged in alphabetical order to make it easier and faster to find the letter required.

2.   A touch screen

This allows the child to use their hands to navigate rather than a mouse which can be distracting. A touch screen teaches a child with ASD about cause and effect, when they touch the screen and a change happens.

3.   A foot mouse

As the name implies, a computer foot mouse enables the user to control the computer mouse using the foot, thus leaving the hands free.

4.   An ergonomic trackball

This is a ball that a child can roll on a desk and which helps to avoid most of the sliding movement of a mouse.

5.   Software

There are many software programs on the market that can help a child with ASD develop different skills. For example:

-    Problem solving skills

-    Communication skills

-    Academic skills

-    Reading skills

Braedan has just recently shown an interest in computers. We are exploring the use of keyboarding for communication now. He will "type" with the keyboard but so far we have not made any words yet. I do believe that he will learn how to do this however and am very excited to see where keyboarding will take us. Right now his favorite thing to do on the computer is to look at pictures of door knobs, which are one of his obsessions.

VIDEO TAPING AND VIDEO MODELING

Video modeling is a teaching technique used to teach children by watching a video where the child can imitate, and observe behavior performed by another child or individual and in doing so, learn a new skill or desirable behavior.

Video modeling is a very effective way to teach children with ASD a new skill because it has been proven to be a faster method of teaching in which ASD grasp the concept faster than if they were taught face to face.

The success of video modeling in teaching skills and target behavior to Autistic children is associated with characteristics common in children on the spectrum such as:

-       Many children with Autism process visual information faster, therefore they learn faster with video modeling.

-       Children with ASD enjoy repetition and video modeling enables the child to review the information over and over again making the skill or desired behavior stick in their memory.

-       It is a safe environment for the child to practice the skill before they have to do it in the real world with people surrounding them. This will greatly reduce the anxiety that the child will feel when they have to try out the skill or behavior in public.

-        Children with ASD do not automatically know how to behave in social settings. Videotaping enables these children to learn social skills at their own pace.

-        After or while viewing the video, a child can then model the behavior or skill they see on tape thus enabling them to gain a new skill.

-        Children with ASD may have sensory issues and using videos can desensitize them towards noisy environments so that when they are in the actual environment the level of noise is tolerable.

SKILLS TAUGHT USING VIDEO TAPING

1.   Language skills

This can be taught through videotaping by naming common objects and names of familiar people and other areas of interest for the child.

2.   Social skills

This is one area where videotaping works very well to impart social skills to children with ASD. Social situations are videotaped and the child can observe how other children behave in such situations.

Children with ASD can also be taught facial expressions, tone of voice, posture, personal space and other areas where the child may be having difficulties.

3.   Self-help skills

Children with ASD can be taught skills such as brushing their teeth, combing their hair, dressing, washing hands and general hygiene through videotaping. They can then mirror the steps on the video and therefore learn a new skill in a fun and non-threatening way.

4.   Academic skills

Children with ASD can improve their academic skills like writing and reading by watching other children writing and reading. The videos also have segments where the child is required to say out loud what they see, thus improving their spoken language too.

Videotaping and video modeling is not a method that I have tried. The research on this does look very promising however. I can see how this method is useful as it is a visual tool that most children with Autism will relate to. If you are currently using this method to teach communication or try it in the future, I would love to know your results.

THE IPAD

Autistic children are drawn to computers and now with the ipad, communication has become more accessible for these children. Children with Autism learn better when they can process the information visually and most communication software is visual making it ideal for these children. An ipad is friendlier to Autistic children because it works via touch screen so there's no need for a mouse which can be distracting for the child.

THE BENEFITS OF USING AN IPAD TO COMMUNICATE

1.   The ipad is easy and light to carry around therefore the Autistic child can have it with him all the time.

2.   No mouse is required and for Autistic children this is a great plus because the distraction of a mouse interferes with their concentration.

3.   ASD children don't like distractions and with an ipad, they don't have to move their eyes from the screen to the keyboard.

4.   A great need for ASD children and adults is predictability. That's why change is so draining for them. With the ipad, there's the comfort of predicting

what will happen when you touch a certain button. All the applications are organized and predictable.

5.   The ipad provides an opportunity for children to learn and also have fun while doing it. They could be doing a fun puzzle and at the same time it's a learning process for the child.

DISADVANTAGES OF THE IPAD

1.   The most glaring disadvantage of the ipad is the cost. Most ipads are very expensive, making them out of reach for many families who cannot afford them.

2.   There's also the worry of your child spending too much time on the ipad. Just like TV, spending too much time on an ipad means that the child is not doing what children should do which is playing. Restricting time spent on the ipad means that your child will get the physical exercise that he needs by playing and running about.

3.   There's also the tendency to use the ipad as a baby-sitting tool. After all, it will keep your child occupied for several hours if you let them. Counter this problem by being actively involved in what your child is doing on the ipad and if possible doing it together.

Braedan is the only one of my sons to use the ipad. He received his first one in 2011. He likes the ipad and has begun to show some success using it. Not only is he beginning to use it to communicate but he has begun to play some of the games that I have downloaded. The problem with Braedan is that when he is done with something he has a tendency to throw it. These devices are quite expensive so I do not allow him to use his unless he is next to me or his one-on-one at school.

Many families cannot afford to buy a new ipad. I have great news for you! There is a new company that not only makes the ipad affordable for everyone they give you 80 different apps to go with it. Puzzle Piece sells the original ipad, in a rubberized case to protect it, for $19. You get to choose from three colors; blue, pink or green. Included with your ipad is access to eighty free apps including, 40 apps for nonverbal communication, forty social stories (more on this in a later chapter) and forty games. The downside to Puzzle Piece is they ask you to sign up for a monthly subscription service which costs $19. So far I have not seen many new apps added that justifies this expense. The upside is you do not have to sign any contracts so you can purchase the ipad, download the free apps then cancel the monthly service.

You can find out more information at their website here: https://www.getpuzzlepiece.com/

Another option for acquiring an ipad for your child is through your caseworker, if you have one. Braedan's caseworker at the Department of Developmental Disabilities denied our request but his caseworker at the mental health agency he was enrolled with provided us the first one. If you are lucky enough to be provided one by either of these types of agencies take very good care of it as it is usually a onetime deal.

SPEECH GENERATING DEVICES

In speech generating devices (SGD), the child with ASD touches a labeled picture or graphic on the screen and the device says the word or sentence out loud. Speech generating devices are said to give a voice to the voiceless.

The computer generated voice can be adapted to a female or male voice or you record the voice that you want it to use. Icons on the device are customized to the child with ASD and they closely mirror their likes and desires. If the child presses the button for I am hungry, a selection will come of foods from his favorite restaurants.

Speech generating devices fall under four categories:

•No tech- this does not require any power source

•Low tech – It is easy to program and requires a source of power

•Mid tech – These devices require a source of power to use. You as the parent have to attend a training session, which usually takes place at the speech therapist office. At this session you will learn how to set up, program and use the device.

•High tech – These are expensive, and require extensive training to use and program. They also require a power source.

SGD'S enhance communication by:

-        Increasing the vocabulary of children with ASD through the use of verbs, describing words and nouns.

-        Clarifying gestures and body language.

-        Associating words with their respective objects thus enabling a child with ASD to know that every object has a name.

-        Helping to develop language

-        Helping nonverbal children have a voice

THE BENEFITS OF SPEECH GENERATING DEVICES (SGD)

1.   SGD's are visual cues which work very well with children on the spectrum who learn better visually.

2.   Autistic children prefer inanimate objects, that is why they are drawn to SGD's

3.   The level of complexity can be adapted to the user therefore these devices are suitable for all ages.

4.   When these devices are introduced to the Autistic child slowly, they do not cause anxiety which many ASD children are prone to.

5.   ASD children exhibit many behavioral issues brought by the inability to communicate their

feelings, wants, needs and even comments. These devices provide an effective way for these children to communicate thereby eliminating most of these challenging behaviors.

6.   Many children with ASD have a problem with memory. Speech generating devices work on recognition rather than memory therefore they are well suited for ASD children.

7.   SGD devices break down social barriers for children with ASD enabling them to communicate with different people that they meet in their daily lives.

8.   SGD also helps with spontaneous communication which many of us enjoy and take for granted. It enables ASD children enjoy unplanned communication and helps their sense of humor to emerge.

9.   These devices foster independence of children with Autism enabling them to function at home, in school and within the community.

10.   SGD devices provide the satisfaction that comes from understanding others and being understood.

Getting one of these for your child is a lot easier than getting an ipad. I am not sure why because these devices are very expensive. Shane had a very basic one and it cost the Department of Developmental Disabilities $1,500. The process can be lengthy but is well worth it. You need to start with a referral from your speech therapist. Once you have the referral give it to your caseworker and they should set up an appointment with a specialist for your child's assessment.

Shane received his assessment for a speech generating device in 2008, when he was nine years old. The assessment itself was very interesting. A team of speech specialists came to visit us with a number of different devices. While one of them asked me questions about Shane's development and abilities to date, the other members of the team assessed his interest and ability to manipulate each device. As explained above, these devices can be extremely simple or very complicated.

Once the team decided which device would work for Shane the order had to be placed with the caseworker. In some cases, this has to be approved by a supervisor so it can take a couple of weeks or a few months to actually receive your device.

Once you receive the device you will be given training on how to set it up and how to use it with your child. This training is usually done at your speech therapist's office. The device that Shane had was fairly simple to set up and use. The one thing I did not like about it was having to change out the screens. For example if he tapped the picture for I'm hungry I would have to remove the screen, put in the pictures for his favorite snacks and he would need to touch another picture. However, if what he wanted was not on that screen I would have to change it again. There were many times when he and I both became frustrated with the process.

MUSIC BASED THERAPY

Music really does soothe the savage beast. There were days in my home when one, or more, of my sons were having a complete meltdown. It seems that if one was having a bad day it wasn't long before they all were. Multiple meltdowns could consist of Stephan banging his head off a wall while screaming. Shane was usually rocking in a corner trying to get away from it all. And Braedan would be following me around growling and clapping his hands at me. Not a fun time for any of us. I very quickly learned that by playing a soothing CD, my family loves Celtic music, I could eliminate all of the tension at once. Within five minutes of starting the CD, Stephan would be sitting on the couch rocking to the music, Shane would be happily dancing a little jig and Braedan would be close by simply listening to the music.

Children with ASD have been shown to respond well to music. Most children on the spectrum have trouble communicating with speech yet they do manage to sing.

Music therapy is done by trained professionals and they structure lessons to teach social skills, communication skills, reading skills, mathematics and other areas.

Research shows that children on the spectrum show a lot of behavior improvement when they are taught using musical approaches.

THE BENEFITS OF MUSIC TO NONVERBAL KIDS

1.   Music is a fun and enjoyable way to learn. Children with ASD have a short attention span however, the fun nature of music enables them to concentrate for longer periods of time.

2.   Music is considered a language that everybody understands and this includes children on the spectrum. Because of this, it helps Autistic children bond and establish emotional connections with people through the shared love of music.

3.   The rhythmic and repetitive nature of music enables children with ASD to calm down. Used as a background in a class, it provides a non-threatening environment for the child thus enabling them to learn better.

4.   Music therapy increases social skills. Children show more emotion during music therapy and they have been shown to respond to their therapists better when there's music involved.

5.   Music has been shown to improve behavior in ASD children. There's less aggression in these children as well as less restlessness.

6.   During music therapy, music is paired with action and this improves the nonverbal child's understanding of verbal commands.

7.   Music therapy helps the ASD child express emotions nonverbally.

8.   It helps to improve social skills by working to increase eye contact and other nonverbal cues.

9.   It improves sensory skills like touch, listening and general awareness of surroundings.

10.   Improves cognitive skills like concentration and attention.

CASE STUDY: NOAH

Noah was slow in reaching all his milestones and when he was twenty four months old, he was diagnosed with Autism. Noah was completely nonverbal and communicated mostly through pointing and most times just having meltdowns due to this lack of communication. His family felt isolated from him as he grew older and more withdrawn.

His meltdowns were increasing and it was becoming more difficult to control him or even understand what he wanted.

When he was six, a friend suggested music therapy for Noah, and though skeptical, his parents decided to give it a try. They enrolled him at a music school nearby that had therapists who specialized in nonverbal children.

To the delight of his parents, Noah took an instant love to music and they have watched the little boy transform day after day. He loves playing musical instruments and surprisingly he seems to have a natural gift for music. Noah has a beautiful singing voice, which is nothing like his voice when he utters a few words.

Four years later, Noah can write music with the help of his music therapist and can hold simple conversations, something his parents and doctors thought he would never be able to do. His confidence has increased so much that he sings at school for students and parents when there's a function at school.

Just recently I discovered a new music therapy for children on the spectrum. I purchased it for my son Braedan. We are not very far into the program but already I have seen positive results in his anxiety levels. The program was designed by a graduate of Julliard School of Music. The program is called The Brain Rhythms Development System. This system is composed of six components used to help your child with social, behavioral and cognitive development. You can find out more information on their website: http://theautismanswer.com/embracing-autism-brain-rhythms-special-parents-offer/

SPEECH THERAPY

Speech and language pathologists help children on the spectrum talk, understand and communicate better with people around them. They don't necessarily focus on talking but they look for different ways in which a child can best communicate.

The speech problems associated with Autism include:

- Echolalia (repeating what another person says and not necessarily understanding the meaning behind the words.)

- Using robotic speech

- Talking using the correct words but the tone does not match the meaning of the words.

- The child does not talk at all

- Word like sounds but cannot be understood.

- Grunts, shrieks and other worrying noises.

- Talking in a musical way

Speech language therapists help nonverbal children with ASD to work through these speech problems with the goal of enabling the child to communicate either verbally or nonverbally.

SPEECH THERAPY IDEAS FOR PARENTS AT HOME

There are ways that you as a parent can help your child on the spectrum improve their speech and communication. The thing to note here is that you should not pressure your child into responding or be angry if they are unable to respond. Be patient, ASD children take a while to learn.

Some of these ideas are:

1.   Place objects that your child uses regularly slightly out of reach but somewhere where they can see it. To get the item your child must use some kind of sign or gesture such as pointing for them to get that object. It will take some time before they can successfully do this, so be patient and don't have high expectations for immediate response.

2.   Children with ASD thrive on routine. Incorporate routines in your everyday activities. For example, when playing on swings, hold the swing and count to three, then say go. After a while, count to three and wait for the child to say go then let go of the swing.

3.   Many parents first realize that their child has a problem due to their lack of response. You'll call out your child's name and they will not respond at all or even show a sign that they recognize their name. When your child responds to their name, reward them with a small treat and show your happiness that they

have responded through positive words and words of affirmation.

4.   Children with ASD tend to have special interest on certain objects, maybe toys, animals etc. Use that special interest to teach your child noises. For example if they are fascinated by animals, teach them the different noises that different animals make.

5.   Involve yourself in your child's play. For example, if they are playing with a train, take a turn, while teaching them the words 'my turn' .It will teach your child to ask for something when they want it.

6.   Children love pretend games and they are a great way for ASD children to learn social skills. Examples of pretend games include a visit to the doctor, playing house, playing shopping etc. These games will help your child interact and bond with other kids his age.

7.   Practice nonverbal communication with your child such as facial expressions, body language, posture etc. This can help your child to communicate his feelings to others. You could teach crossing hands over the chest as a sign of dissatisfaction, nodding and shaking the head to indicate yes or no etc.

8.   Teach your child about feelings. If your child has a certain book that he loves, use it to teach him to identify feelings. Look for happy and smiling faces and label it so that he can associate the name with the feeling. Reinforce this by copying the expression

yourself. Show him a sad face on his favorite book and also look sad for him whilst repeating the word.

9.   There are numerous opportunities at home to teach a child with ASD to ask questions. Start with simple questions like what is this, and gradually add on to that.

10.   Enlist members of your family to enact social situations. You could reenact being in a playground or simply an interaction of kids. Another idea would be reenact being in a class. You could be the teacher and the rest, including your child, could be pupils.

These therapy ideas sound simple on paper but they are difficult on a day to day basis. Sometimes you will work with your child for days and even weeks and get no response. It will be disheartening and discouraging. But one day when you least expect it, you'll get a response from your child and all those hours will be worth it.

The milestones are few and far between but when you reach them, the hours you spent teaching your child will fade. All you will remember will be the sound of his voice asking what this is or him leading you by the arm to point at something that he wants.

All three of my sons participated in speech therapy. Your child will be given speech therapy at school but do not stop there. In most cases, the school based therapy sessions are done in a group. These sessions focus on a generalized curriculum and does not touch on your individual child's needs. You should seek out professional speech therapy. If your family is enrolled in the Developmental Disabilities Program, the name differs by state but every state has one, they will provide these services to your child. A standard session takes about one hour once a week. Your speech therapist can also be a great resource for ideas of activities that you can do at home to encourage communication with your child.

OTHER WAYS OF COMMUNICATING WITH YOUR NONVERBAL CHILD

1.   Use of puppets – Children who are nonverbal have been found to communicate with puppets. Introduce your child to puppets and show him how to play with them. Children on the spectrum delight in puppets because they are non-threatening and they can control what the puppets say and when they say it.

2.   Make flashcards of your child's favorite toys, friends, family members and pictures of the child's favorite objects. Laminate them and have them close to the child. Point out the people and objects while saying their names.

3.   Use objects of reference to help your child know what activity they are about to partake in. For example an object of reference for eating may be a spoon. When you show your child a spoon they automatically know that it is meal time.

4.   Communication passport – this is a one page document with all the basic information relating to your child. The purpose of this is to let people who come into contact with your child know how they communicate and the support they will need from the people around them.

5.   Social stories – They are an effective way to teach social and communication skills to children on

the spectrum. Social stories were created by Carol Gray in 1991 and they are short descriptions of activities and events and specific information on what to expect during that situation and why.

Social stories help a child to:

-        Complete tasks that they do not like performing.

-        Increase their independence

-        Teach abstract concepts like time,

-        Improve a child's behavior during transition times

As a writer, I love social stories. You can do a search online to find a number of websites where you can download them, but it is more fun to create your own. I use social stories to help Braedan understand what will happen when we go to the doctors, dentist, or other activities that cause him to feel anxious. I read them before we go plus we read them again while in the waiting room, or standing in line etc. If you are interested in personalized social stories featuring your child, send me an email.

6.   Incorporate other means of expression – People express themselves through different ways like singing, drawing, painting, dancing etc. Incorporate these activities into your child's routine to give them more opportunities to express them.

7.   Try mirrors – Children with ASD don't like eye contact, probably because it is draining and also to avoid sensory overload. To train your child to make eye contact, you can use mirrors to see if they feel comfortable looking at you that way.

8.   Talk to them anyway – Even if your child is nonverbal, talk to them anyway. It does not mean that because they don't speak they have a problem with their hearing. Talking to them, will enable them to know names of thing and also say a few words themselves. It's also important to not speak about your nonverbal child when they are in the room. Autistic children who have grown and found a way to communicate say that it' very hurtful for them when their family members and friends speak about them as if they are not there.

9.   Treat all nonverbal actions from your child as if they have meaning and work hard to find out what your child is trying to communicate. Let every opportunity be a way for your child to communicate and be understood.

10.   Make the nonverbal cues that your child can do mean something. For example a clap could mean no. Over time you'll have amassed nonverbal signs that will enable your child to express their needs and communicate if they have a problem.

NAVIGATING THE LAND OF AUTISM

Just because they don't talk doesn't mean that they don't feel. Children with ASD have the same needs as the rest of the population and they require a means to let these needs and desires be known. Communication is the biggest challenge for children with Autism.

Some of these children can't speak and are unable to interpret gestures and facial expressions and we know that despite people communicating verbally, a lot of information is exchanged nonverbally.

Children with ASD have been labeled as rude and their parents accused of not disciplining their children. As if dealing with the many challenges that come with parenting ASD children is not enough, these parents also have to face a judgmental society. Raising awareness is important because it provides information to the general public about these special members of our society. People on the spectrum have to learn painstakingly slow the skills most of us are born with and take for granted.

They have to learn how to communicate without using words; they are expected to know how to behave in different situations all the while dealing with sensory sensitivities. Some hear every day noises as very loud, comparing the humming of the fridge to a dentist drilling into their mouths.

Another child will be bothered by smells, even perfumes and colognes and strong smelling places like fish mongers etc.

As a parent of a child with ASD, you never know what might set that child off. We hope that this book has shown you that your child does not mean to annoy you or to gain attention. Their behavior, however disruptive is a means of communicating - Possibly their only means of communication.

These children do not have the words to express their needs and desires, so they use their behavior to communicate. It is up to the parents and caregivers to interpret the meaning behind these behaviors. Your child could be hungry, suffering from a sensory overload and needing a quiet space, could be in physical pain, could even be having an undiagnosed seizure and the list goes on.

In these modern times there are numerous technological devices that can help nonverbal children to communicate and even learn to interact with others. There's the PEC system which has proven to be very successful with Autistic children, the use of computers to learn and communicate, speech generating devices and many more. They can facilitate learning in your child with ASD.

Children on the spectrum have gone on to be independent people who are successful in their chosen careers. It is a huge but rewarding job, parents and these children need encouragement and help along the way. We hope that this book has done that and showed you, the parent, that it can be done and that there's a whole world out there open for your child on the spectrum.

Once you understand how to connect and communicate with your tour guide, navigating the land of Autism becomes so much easier. You will be able to eliminate many of the challenging behaviors and stress from their lives and yours. Teaching other skills, like hygiene and chores becomes quicker and easier to do. Not only do you need to teach your child to communicate with you but you need to learn how to retrain yourself to communicate with them. Be patient with you and your child, this is not an easy task. Reward yourselves when progress is made and do not beat yourselves up when it seems as if you will never get "it".

REFERENCES:

Autism Speaks

11 Myths About Autsim

http://blog.autismspeaks.org/2011/11/21/11-myths-about-autism/

National Autism Association

Autism Fact Sheet

http://nationalautismassociation.org/resources/autism-fact-sheet/

ABOUT THE AUTHOR

Shawna Sparlin is a single mom, author and writer living in Tennessee. Her writing resume includes website content, copywriting, resumes, press releases, articles, and ebooks. Shawna's favorite topics to write about, tips for other parents on raising children with Autism (she has 3 boys with Autism), gardening, natural healing, and Wicca. She has four other published ebooks, Magick of Love, 25 All Natural Cough & Cold Remedies, Younger Skin in 30 Days or Less and Eat Your Anxiety Before it Eats You.

Shawna has dreamt of being a writer since she could hold a pencil, entertaining her mother and sisters with poems and stories for years. She took up writing professionally six years ago. When she is not busy writing she spend her time with her youngest son and working to help other independent authors promote their work.

Contact information:

You can send an email to magickmompress@gmail.com or

Visit my website: www.magickmom.com

www.ingramcontent.com/pod-product-compliance
Lightning Source LLC
Chambersburg PA
CBHW060950040426

42445CB00011B/1085